Let's Classify and Fold Origami Animals

Let's Classify and Fold ORIGAMI BIRDS

by Ruth Owen

Enslow PUBLISHING

Published in 2023 by Enslow Publishing, LLC
29 East 21st Street, New York, NY 10010

Produced for Rosen by Ruth Owen Books
Designer: Emma Randall
Photos courtesy of Ruth Owen Books and Shutterstock

Cataloging-in-Publication Data

Names: Owen, Ruth.
Title: Let's classify and fold origami birds / Ruth Owen.
Description: New York : Enslow Publishing, 2023. | Series: Let's classify and fold origami animals | Includes glossary and index.
Identifiers: ISBN 9781978530065 (pbk.) | ISBN 9781978530089 (library bound) | ISBN 9781978530072 (6pack) | ISBN 9781978530096 (ebook)
Subjects: LCSH: Birds in art--Juvenile literature. | Origami--Juvenile literature.
Classification: LCC TT872.5 O937 2023 | DDC 736'.982--dc23

Manufactured in the United States of America

CPSIA compliance information: Batch #CSENS23: For further information contact Enslow Publishing LLC, New York, New York at 1-800-398-2504.

Contents

Meet the Birds

Birds come in many shapes and colors. They also range in size from the tiny bee hummingbird, that's just 2 inches (5 cm) long, to an ostrich that can grow to be 9 feet (3 m) tall! There are more than 10,000 different **species**, or types, of birds.

Birds have six main characteristics.

Birds have wings and most species are able to fly. Some types of birds, such as ostriches and penguins, are flightless, however.

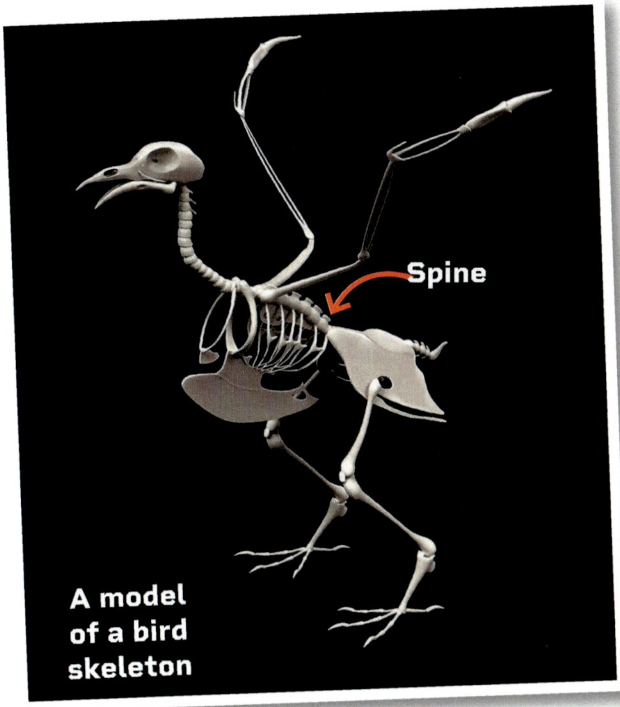

A model of a bird skeleton

Birds are **vertebrates**, which means they have a spine, or backbone. Most birds have a lightweight skeleton which reduces their body weight for flying.

Macaw parrot

Birds are **endothermic**, or warm-blooded. This means a bird's body is able to **regulate** its inner body temperature. Even if its environment is very hot or cold, a bird's inner body temperature stays the same.

Robin eggs inside a nest

All birds have beaks and feathers.

No matter how big or small, every bird begins its life by hatching from an egg.

Ready to discover more? Then grab some origami paper and let's get folding and learning all about birds!

A Bird's Life Cycle: Chicks and Eggs

The life cycle of every bird on Earth begins with an egg. The chicks of some bird species, for example robins and owls, are helpless when they hatch from their eggs. The baby birds cannot walk or see. Their parents must bring them food for the first few weeks of their lives. Other chicks, such as the babies of ducks, ostriches, and chickens, can run around and peck at food within a day of hatching.

Just as birds come in many sizes, so do their eggs. The eggs of the tiny bee hummingbird are smaller than an M&M. The largest egg is laid by the ostrich. It can weigh more than 3 pounds (1.4 kg)!

FOLD A HATCHING CHICK

You will need:

- A square piece of paper that's yellow on one side and white on the other
- A black marker

STEP 1:

Place the paper colored side down, fold in half diagonally, and crease. Then fold in half again.

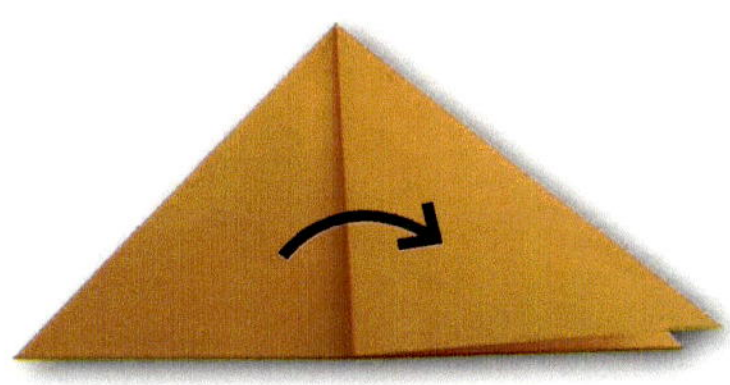

STEP 2:

Turn the paper so the longest side is at the bottom. Fold the top flap of the paper back on itself, and crease.

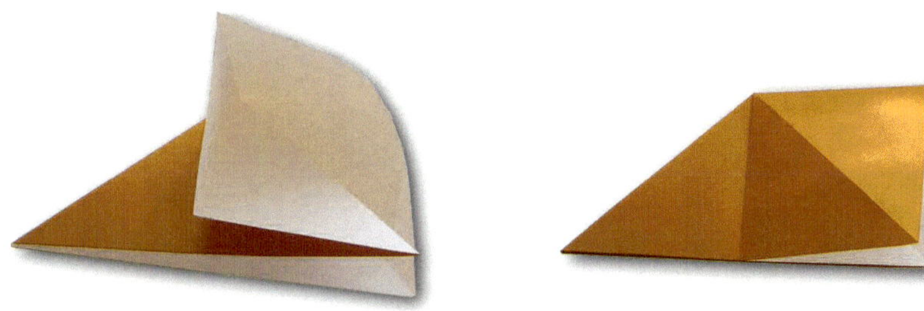

STEP 3:

Now open out the top pocket of paper on the right side. Gently squash the pocket and fold it back down to form a square.

STEP 4:

Turn the model over. Now fold in the right side along the dotted line, and crease. Open out the top pocket of paper and then gently squash and fold it back down to form a square.

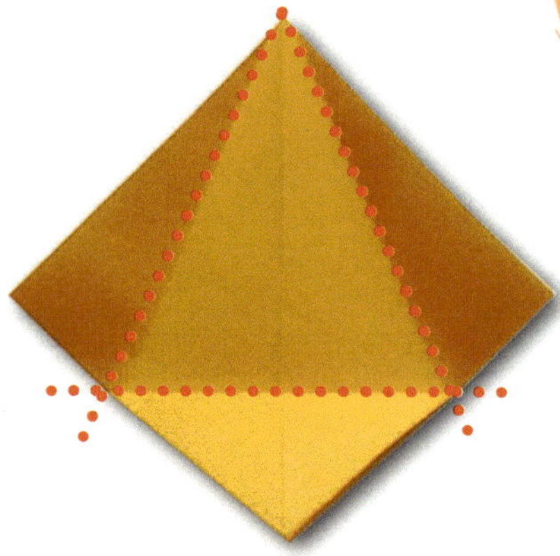

STEP 5:

Turn the model so that the open points are at the top. Fold both sides and the bottom into the center along the dotted lines, and crease. Then unfold.

STEP 6:

Now pull open the top layer of paper. Then gently squash it back down to form a diamond shape, and crease.

STEP 7:

Fold up the bottom point of the diamond so it lays flat against the model.

STEP 8:

Turn the model over. Fold down the top layer of paper, and crease. Your model should look like this.

STEP 9:

Now fold down the two points at the top of the model to make the chick's wings, and crease.

STEP 10:
Fold the three points behind the model, along the dotted lines, and crease.

STEP 11:
Fold down the top point to make the chick's head.

STEP 12:
Finally make two small folds at the pointed end of the chick's head to create its beak. Fold back the corners of its head to round off the shape.

Draw on eyes, and your hatching chick is complete!

Tiny Nectar Drinkers: Hummingbirds

Hummingbirds feed on nectar from flowers using their long beaks and tongues. To do this, they must hover in front of a flower. The ruby-throated hummingbird beats its wings about 50 times each second as it hovers!

Ruby-throated hummingbird

FOLD A HUMMINGBIRD

You will need:

- A square piece of paper in your choice of color
- Scissors

Step 1:

To begin making your hummingbird, follow steps 1 to 4 of the chick and egg project on page 7. Your model should now look like this.

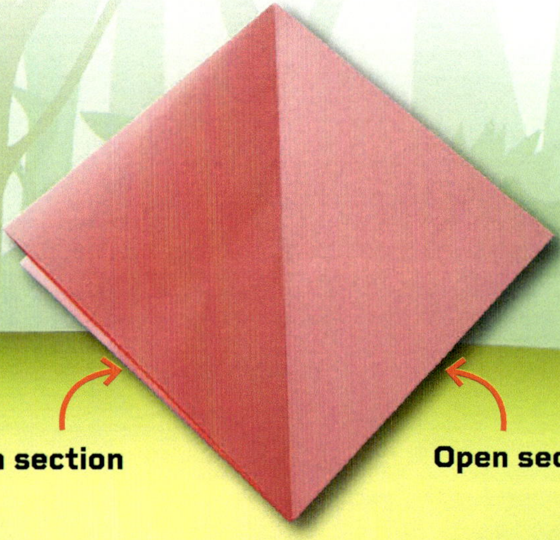

Step 2:

Working with just the top layers of paper, fold the two side points into the center, and crease hard.

Step 3:

Turn the model over and repeat step 2. Next, fold down the top point, and crease hard.

A view from the side of the model

Step 4:

Now unfold the three folds you made in step 3 and open up the top layer of paper. Your model will look a little like a bird's beak.

Next, gently squash and flatten the model to create a diamond shape.

Turn the model over and it should look like this.

Step 5:
Now repeat what you did in step 4, unfolding the top layer of paper, and then squashing and flattening the paper into a diamond shape.

You should now have two leg-like points at the bottom of your model.

Step 6:
Turn the model 90 degrees clockwise. Working with just the top layer of paper, fold up the bottom point into the center.

Then turn the model over and fold up the bottom point.

Now, working with just the top layer of paper, fold down the top point.

Finally, turn the model over and fold down the remaining top point.

Step 7:
Turn the model so the two leg-like points are at the bottom.

Leg-like points

Next, fold up the left-hand point. Crease hard and then unfold.

Step 7 continued:

Now slightly open out the left-hand side of the model. Using the folds you've just made, reverse fold the left-hand point up and tuck it inside the model.

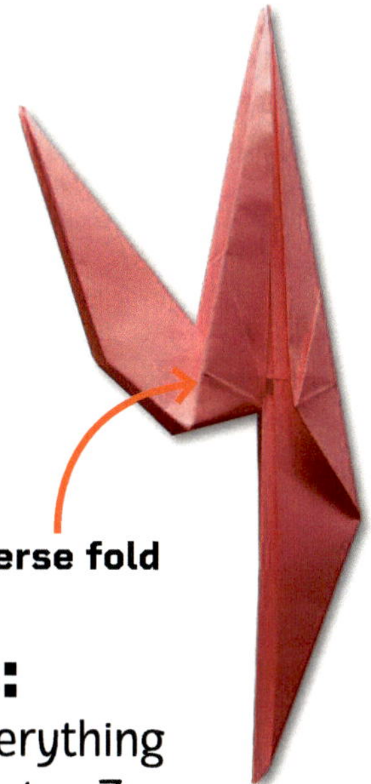

Step 8:

Repeat everything you did in step 7 on the right-hand point of the model.

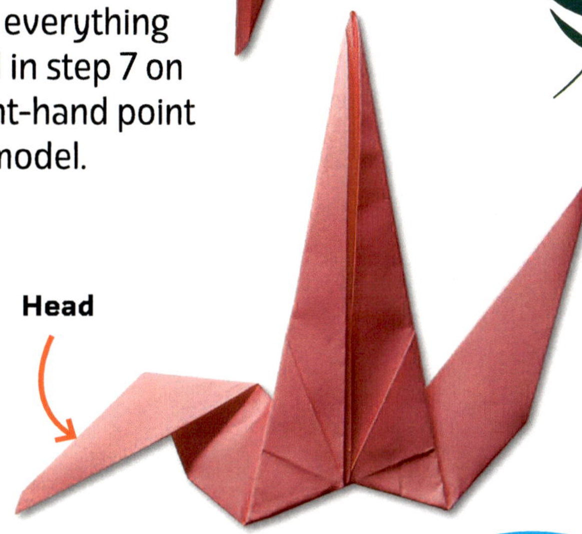

Step 9:

Next, to create the hummingbird's head, fold down the left-hand point, crease hard, and then unfold.

Using the folds you've just made, reverse fold the head section.

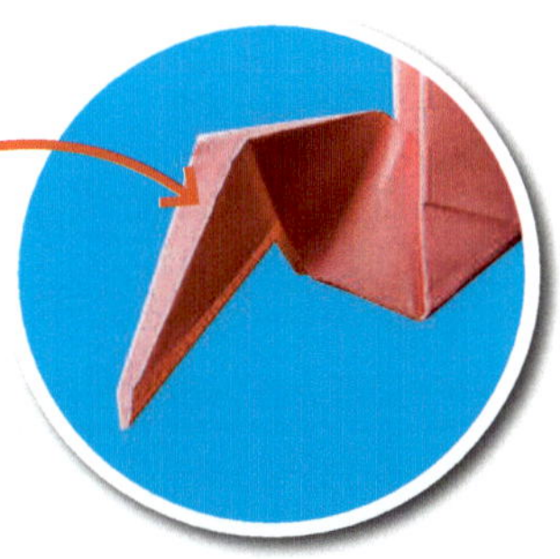

Now twist and squeeze the point to create the bird's long beak and head.

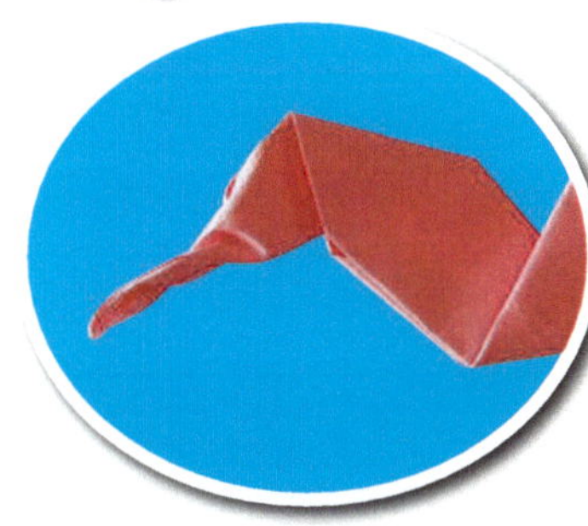

Step 10:

To make the bird's tail, fold down the left-hand point of the model, crease hard, and then unfold.

Using the folds you've just made, reverse fold the tail.

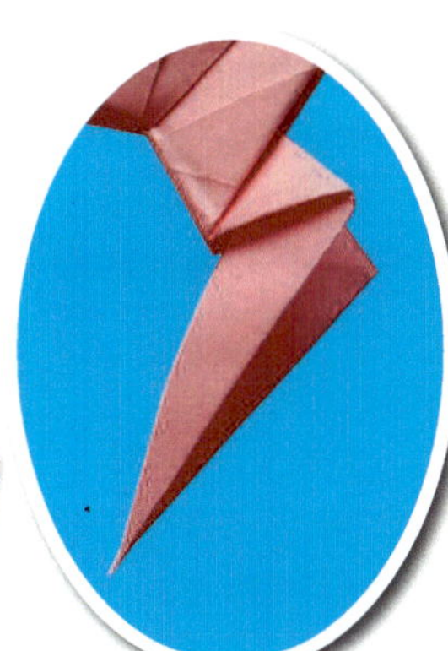

To help the bird's tail fan out, trim off the tip and cut feathers into the fan.

Meet the Raptors: Bald Eagles

Birds that hunt, such as owls and eagles, are known as raptors or birds of **prey**. These highly skilled hunters capture and eat **rodents** and other small mammals, fish, and smaller birds.

Bald eagles are large, powerful hunters that catch fish, **waterfowl**, squirrels, rabbits, and raccoons. They grab their prey with their feet. Then they kill it by crushing it with their sharp **talons**. An eagle eats every part of its prey including bones, feathers, or fur. After its meal, the bird **regurgitates** the fur and any other bits that its digestive system cannot break down.

FOLD A BALD EAGLE

You will need:

- A square piece of paper that's black on one side and white on the other

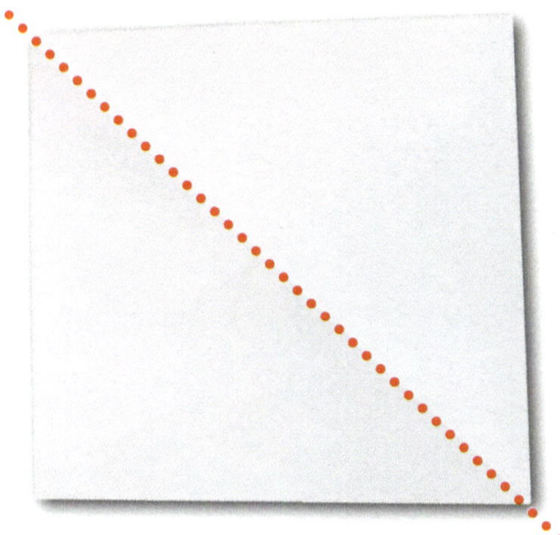

STEP 1:

Place the paper black side down, fold along the dotted line, crease, and unfold.

STEP 2:

Fold the two side points into the center, and crease.

STEP 3:

Fold the top point back behind the model, and crease.

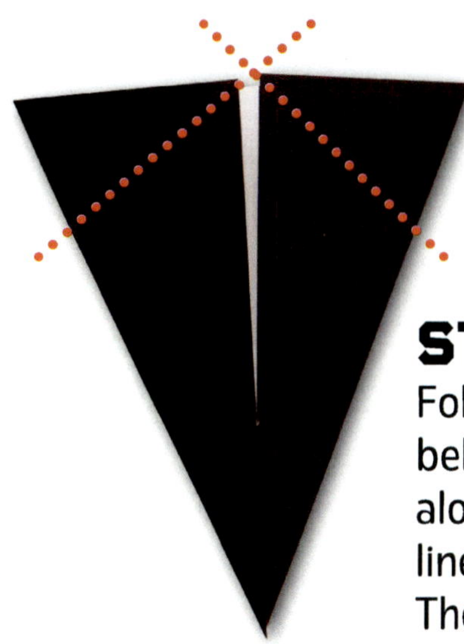

STEP 4:

Fold the two sides behind the model along the dotted lines, and crease. Then unfold again.

STEP 5:

Now lift up point A. Gently fold and squash the paper down so it creates a diamond shape, and crease well.

STEP 6:

Now repeat step 5 on the other side. Your model should look like this.

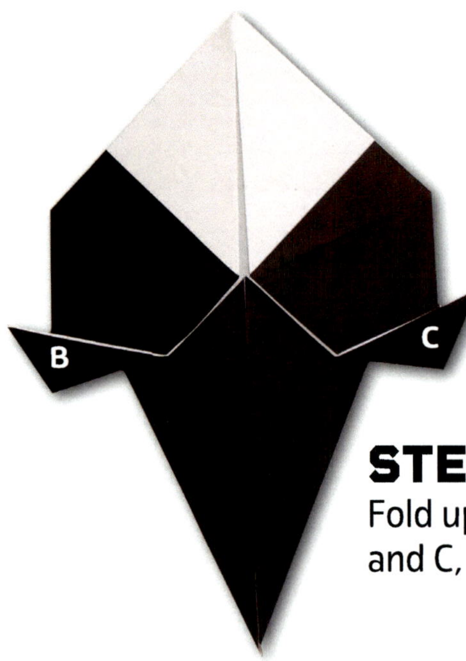

STEP 7:

Fold up points B and C, and crease.

STEP 8:

Now close up the model along its center fold. The model should look like this.

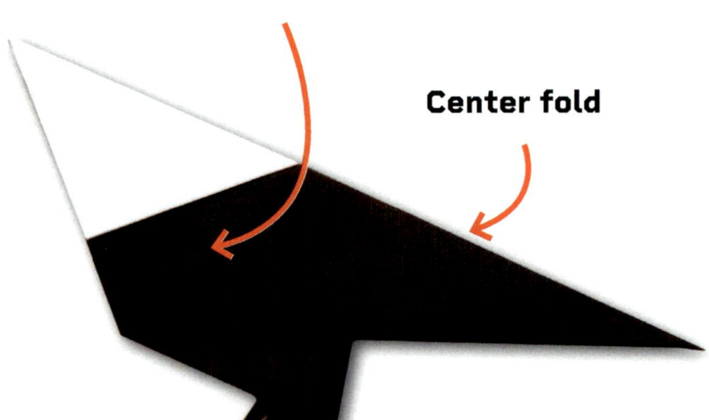

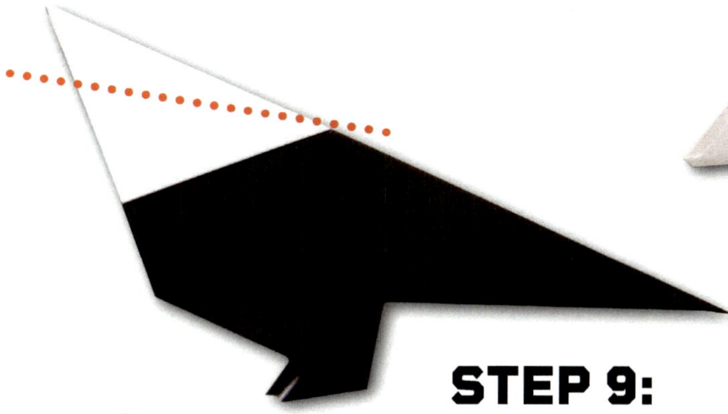

STEP 9:

Fold the white part of the model backward along the dotted line to make the eagle's head, and crease.

STEP 10:

Fold the eagle's tail behind the model, and crease. The back of the model should look like this.

STEP 11:

Now fold the tail back in the other direction to create a small pleat, and crease.

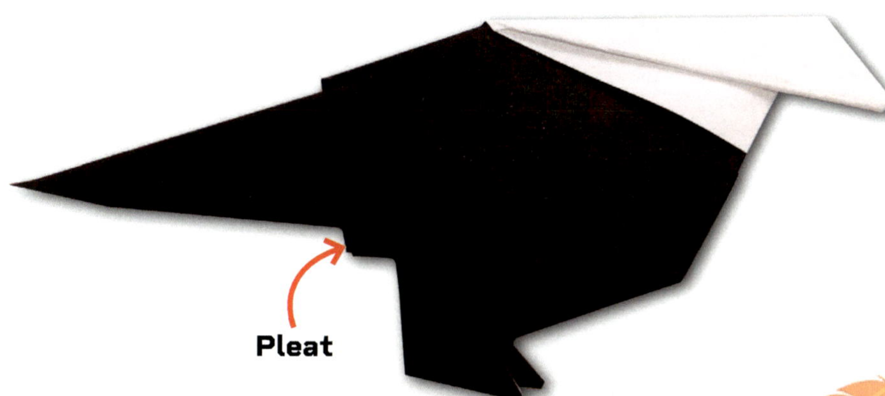

STEP 12:

Turn the model over again, and your bald eagle is complete!

A Rainbow of Feathers: Parrots

Every bird, big or small, dull or colorful, has feathers covering its body and wings. Feathers keep birds warm and dry, and help them fly.

Macaws are large parrots with very brightly colored feathers. When a macaw chick hatches from its egg, however, it is covered in pale, fluffy feathers called down. During its first few weeks, though, the chick loses its down and small spikes, called pin feathers, start to grow. Then, red, blue, yellow, or green feathers soon **unfurl** from the pin feathers.

FOLD A PARROT

You will need:

- A square piece of colorful paper
- Scissors

Step 1:

Fold the paper in half, crease well, and then unfold. Fold the paper in half again, in the opposite direction, crease well, and then unfold.

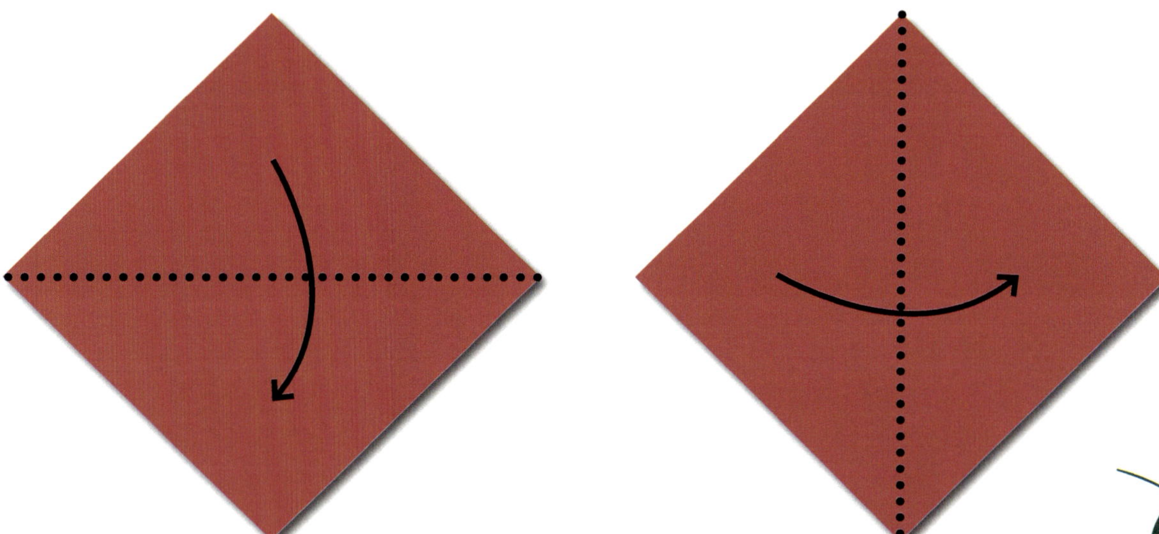

Step 2:

Fold the top and bottom points into the center crease along the dotted lines. Crease well, and then unfold.

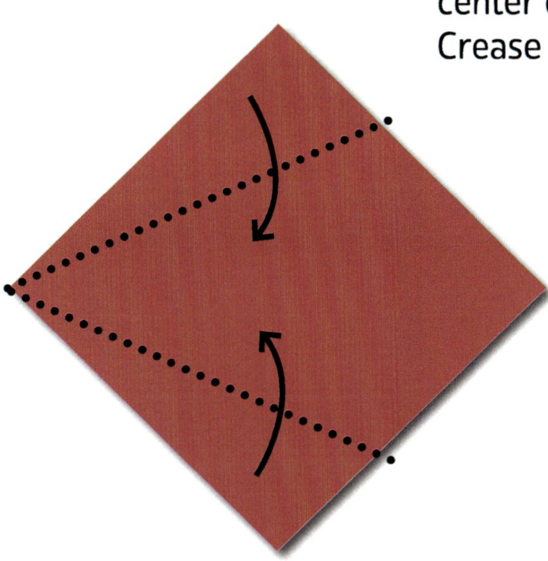

Step 3:

Now fold the top and bottom points into the center crease in the opposite direction. Crease well, and then unfold.

Step 4:

Now gently fold the top half of the paper into the center crease while allowing the top point to create a beak-like pocket. Then squash the pocket and fold it to the right-hand side of the model.

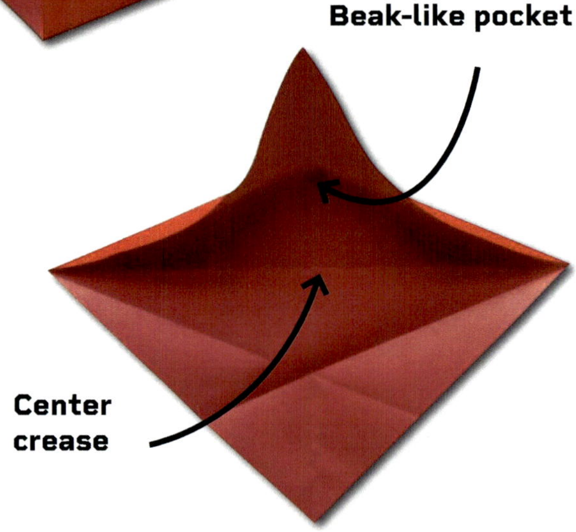

Repeat on the bottom half of the model.

Step 5:

Turn the model over. Fold down the top half along the center crease.

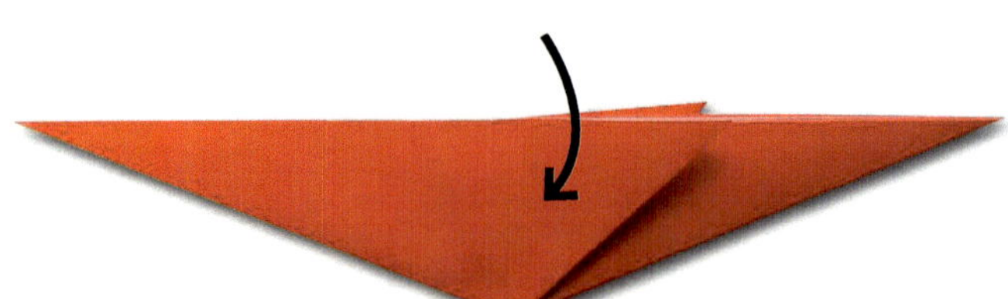

Step 6:

Turn the model by 90 degrees clockwise. To make the parrot's head, fold down the top point, crease well, and then unfold.

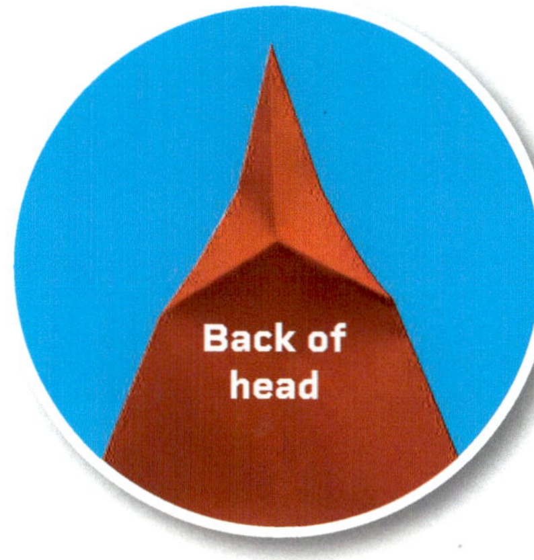

Open out the head section of the model.

Then reverse fold the head using the creases you've just made. Your parrot's head should now look like this.

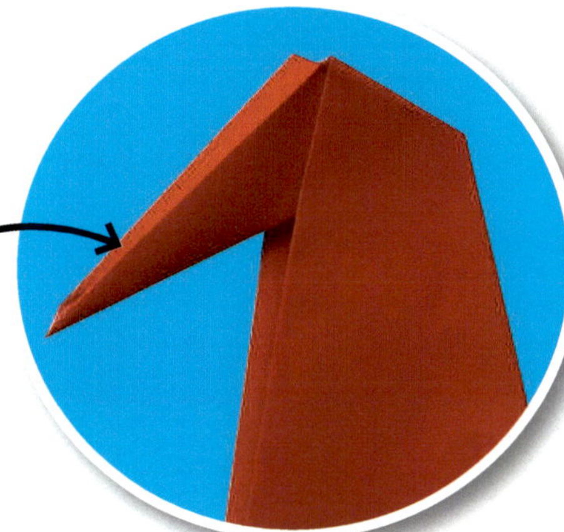

Step 7:

Fold down the tip of the head to make the parrot's beak.

Step 8:

To complete the parrot, cut some feather shapes into the parrot's tail.

Feathers for Finding Mates: Turkeys

Often male birds are more colorful than their female partners. Some male birds have special feathers for showing off to females during the **mating season**.

Turkeys are large birds that live wild in forests. When a male turkey wants to impress a female, he struts toward her and makes gobbling noises. He also puffs out the feathers on his body. His long tail feathers fan out to create a dramatic display.

FOLD A TURKEY

You will need:
- Two square pieces of paper in your choice of colors
- Scissors
- Glue or tape

STEP 1:
To make the turkey's body, fold a piece of paper in half diagonally, crease, and unfold.

STEP 2:
Now fold the two side points in so they meet in the center, and crease well.

STEP 3:
Repeat Step 2 by folding both sides of the model into the center again, and crease well.

STEP 4:
Turn the model over. Fold down the top point to meet the bottom of the model, and crease.

Then fold the point back up again to create the turkey's head.

STEP 5:

Now turn the model by 90 degrees.
Fold the model in half by bringing together points A and B behind the model.

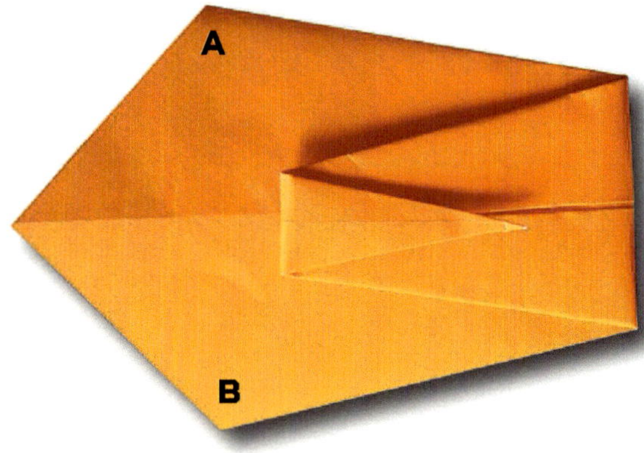

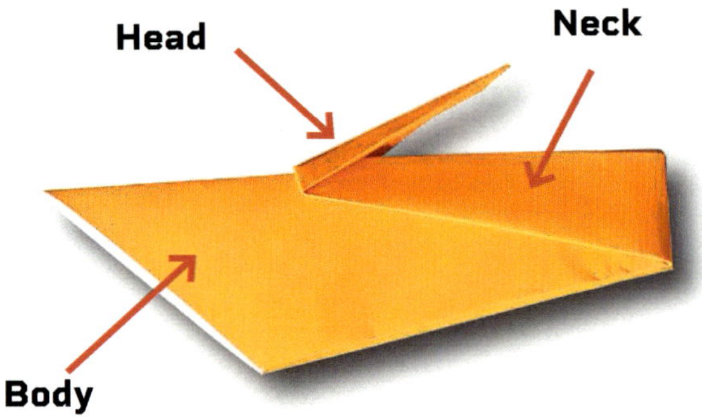

Then gently pull up the neck part of the model.

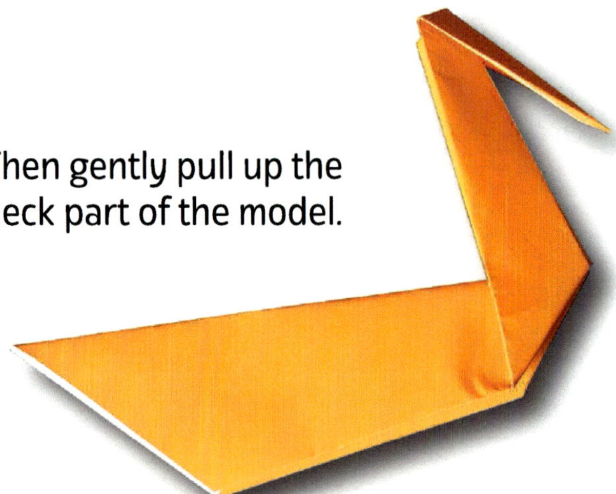

STEP 6:

Fold down the point of the turkey's head to make its wobbly wattle.

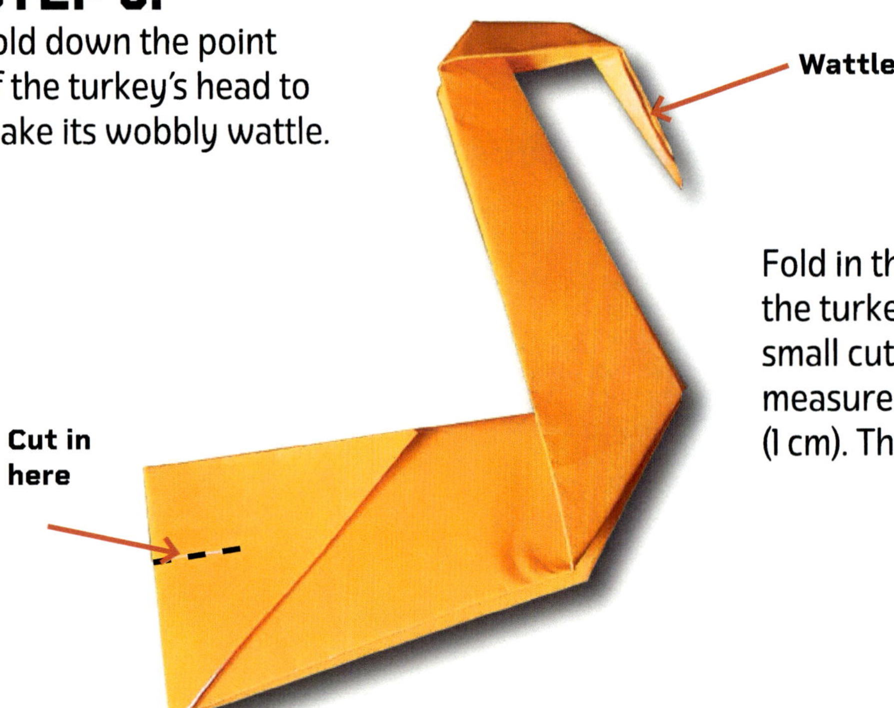

Fold in the left-hand side of the turkey's body. Make a small cut into the body that measures about 1/4 of an inch (1 cm). Then unfold.

STEP 7:

To make the turkey's tail, take the second piece of paper and fold it into a series of pleats. Each pleat should be the width of the cut that's now in the turkey's body.

Once all the pleats are made, gather them together into a narrow bunch. Fold the bunch in half lengthwise.

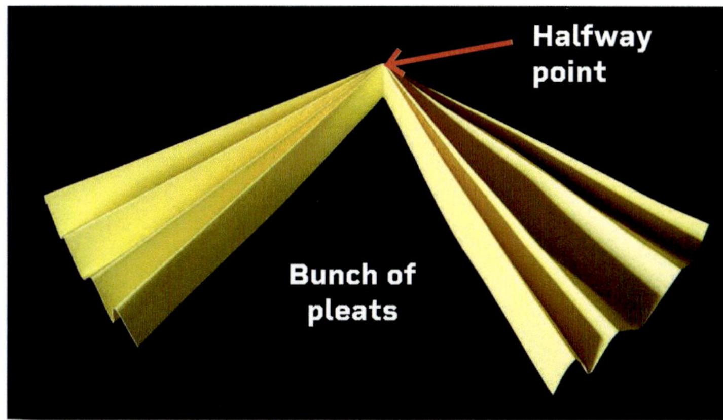

STEP 8:

Now slot the bunch of pleats through the cut in the turkey's body, so that half the pleats are on either side of the body. Adjust the length of the cut if you need to.

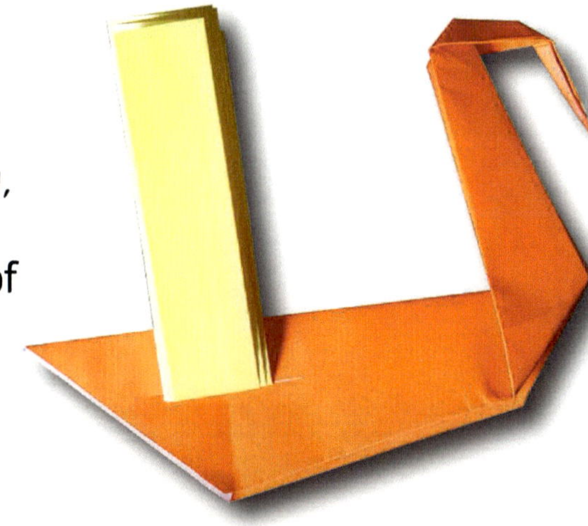

Your model should now look like this.

STEP 9:

Fan out the pleats on either side of the turkey's body. Use a little tape or glue to hold the pleats in the perfect position. Your origami turkey is complete!

Built for the Cold: Emperor Penguins

Emperor penguins have large amounts of body fat and layers of overlapping feathers. They need to be **insulated** against the cold because their Antarctic home is one of the coldest places on Earth. Here, temperatures can drop to -22°F (-30°C). Freezing blizzards blow at more than 100 miles per hour (160 km/h).

After a female emperor lays an egg she heads off to sea to hunt. Her mate **incubates** the egg, keeping it warm on his feet. As they care for their eggs, the thousands of males in a **colony** huddle together to keep warm. They take turns standing on the freezing outside of the huddle and inside the toasty warm center.

FOLD A PENGUIN

You will need:

- A square piece of paper that's black on one side and white on the other

Step 1:
Place the paper white side down. Fold in half diagonally, and crease.

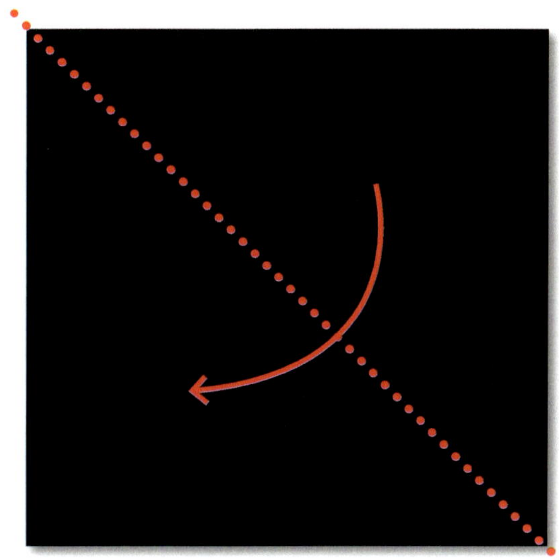

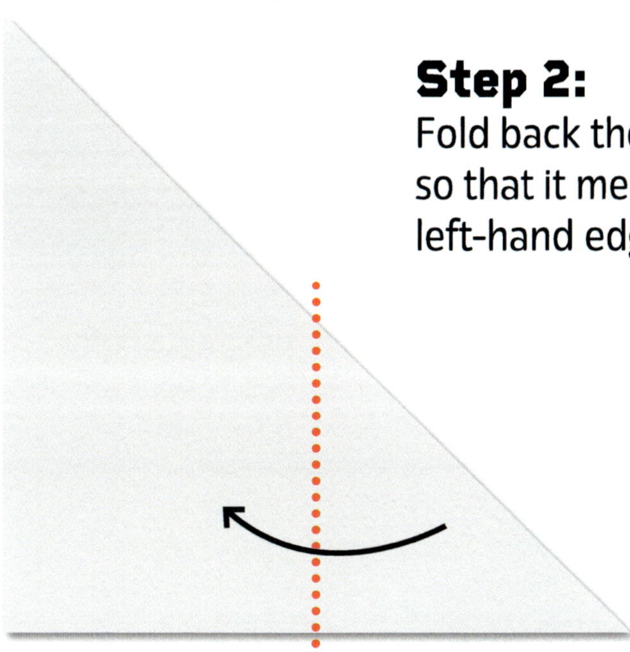

Step 2:
Fold back the right-hand point so that it meets the model's left-hand edge. Crease well.

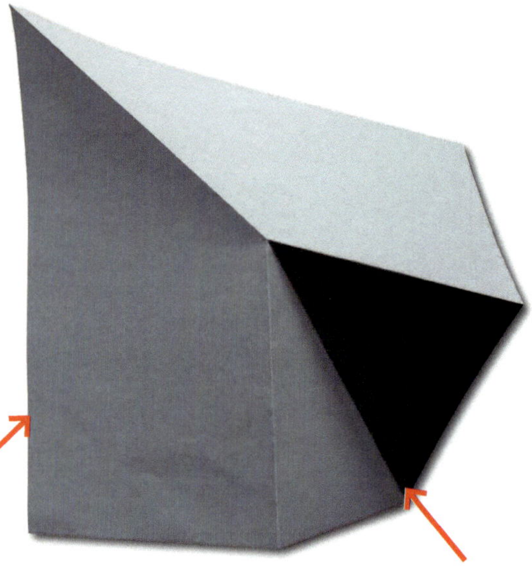

Left-hand edge

Reverse fold the right-hand point of the model

Step 3:

Unfold the crease you've just made. Open out the model, and using the creases you've just made, reverse fold the right-hand point so that it folds inside the model.

The right-hand point is now folded and tucked inside the model.

Step 4:

Now fold the left-hand edge forward along the dotted line, and crease.

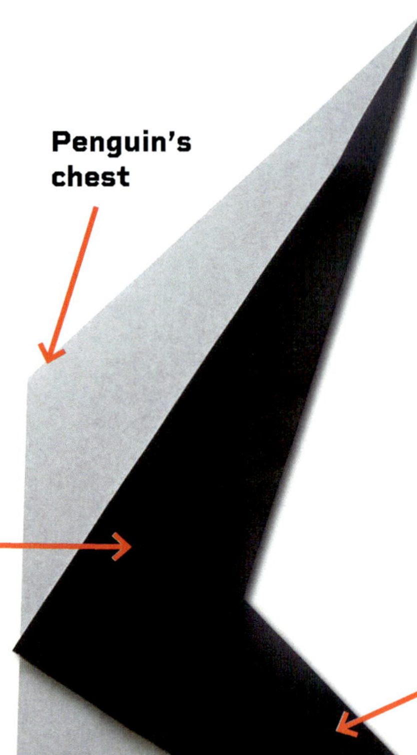

Penguin's chest

Wing

Tail

Step 5:

Turn the model over and repeat step 4. The penguin's body, wings, and tail are now complete.

Step 6:
To make the penguin's head, fold down the top point of the model so that the top edge of the head is parallel to the bottom edge of the model. Crease hard and then unfold.

Open out the head section of the model.

Using the creases you've just made, reverse fold the head so that it folds down over the body. The black hood of the penguin's head should now be tucked around either side of the white chest.

Step 7:
Gently open out the bottom of the model so your penguin can stand, and your model is complete.

Glossary

colony
A large group of animals that live together.

endothermic
Warm-blooded and able to maintain a constant inner body temperature.

incubates
Keeps an egg warm so the chick inside develops and hatches.

insulated
Protected by fat or by layers of material to stop heat loss.

mating season
The time of year when a particular species of animal mates.

prey
An animal that is hunted by another animal as food.

regulate
To adjust the temperature up or down to keep it at the same level.

regurgitates
Coughs up (or vomits up) something that has already been eaten.

rodents
A large group of small animals that includes mice, rats, hamsters, squirrels, and prairie dogs.

species
One type of living thing. The members of a species look alike and can produce young together.

talons
Sharp claws on the feet of a bird of prey, such as an eagle or owl.

unfurl
Spread out from a rolled-up state.

vertebrates
Animals with spines, or backbones, and a skeleton of other bones.

waterfowl
Birds, such as ducks and geese, that spend lots of time on water.

Read More

Allan, John. *Birds (Amazing Life Cycles).* Minneapolis, MN: Hungry Tomato, 2019.

Emminizer, Theresa. *Ostrich: The Largest Bird (Animal Record Breakers).* New York: PowerKids Press, 2020.

Owen, Ruth. *Why Do Birds Have Feathers? (Tell Me More! Science).* Minneapolis, MN: Ruby Tuesday Books, 2021.

Websites

https://www.nwf.org/Educational-Resources/Wildlife-Guide/birds

https://kids.nationalgeographic.com/animals/birds

https://www.audubon.org/bird-guide

Publisher's note to educators and parents: Our editors have carefully reviewed these websites to ensure that they are suitable for students. Many websites change frequently, however, and we cannot guarantee that a site's future contents will continue to meet our high standards of quality and educational value. Be advised that students should be closely supervised whenever they access the internet.

Index